# STONE MILK

# Titles by Anne Stevenson

POETRY

*Living in America* (Generation Press,
  University of Michigan, USA, 1965)
*Reversals* (Wesleyan University Press, USA, 1969)
*Travelling Behind Glass: Selected Poems 1963-1973*
  (Oxford University Press, 1974)
*Correspondences, a Family History in Letters*
  (Oxford University Press, 1974)
*Enough of Green* (Oxford University Press, 1977)
*Sonnets for Five Seasons* (Five Seasons Press, 1979)
*Minute by Glass Minute* (Oxford University Press, 1982)
*A Legacy* (Taxvs Press, 1983)
*The Fiction-Makers* (Oxford University Press, 1985)
*Wintertime* (MidNAG, 1986)
*Selected Poems 1956-1986* (Oxford University Press, 1987)
*The Other House* (Oxford University Press, 1990)
*Four and a Half Dancing Men* (Oxford University Press, 1993)
*The Collected Poems 1955-1995*
  (Oxford University Press, 1996; Bloodaxe Books, 2000)
*Granny Scarecrow* (Bloodaxe Books, 2000)
*A Report from the Border* (Bloodaxe Books, 2003)
*Poems 1955-2005* (Bloodaxe Books, 2005)
*Stone Milk* (Bloodaxe Books, 2007)

LITERARY CRITICISM & BIOGRAPHY

*Elizabeth Bishop* (Twayne, USA, 1966)
*Bitter Fame: A Life of Sylvia Plath*
  (Viking, 1989; Houghton Mifflin, USA, 1989)
*Between the Iceberg and the Ship: Selected Essays*
  (University of Michigan Press, 1998)
*Five Looks at Elizabeth Bishop*
  (Bellew/Agenda Editions, 1998; Bloodaxe Books, 2006)

POETRY CASSETTE

*The Poetry Quartets 6* (The British Council/Bloodaxe Books, 2000)
[shared with Moniza Alvi, Michael Donaghy, Anne Stevenson and George Szirtes]

*Anne Stevenson*

# STONE MILK

## BLOODAXE BOOKS

ISBN: 978 1 85224 775 1

First published 2007 by
Bloodaxe Books Ltd,
Highgreen,
Tarset,
Northumberland NE48 1RP.

www.bloodaxebooks.com
For further information about Bloodaxe titles
please visit our website or write to
the above address for a catalogue.

Bloodaxe Books Ltd acknowledges
the financial assistance of
Arts Council England, North East.

Cover design: Neil Astley & Pamela Robertson-Pearce.

Cover printing: J. Thomson Colour Printers Ltd, Glasgow.

Printed in Great Britain by
Bell & Bain Limited, Glasgow, Scotland.

*In loving memory of*
SUSAN COOPER
(1935-2006)

# ACKNOWLEDGEMENTS

*A Lament for the Makers* was first published in August 2006 in a special edition of 200 copies by Andrew McNeillie's Clutag Press in Thame, Oxfordshire. 'Stone Milk', 'The Enigma', 'Orcop' and 'Inheriting my Grandmother's Nightmare' have appeared in *Poetry* (Chicago). 'Near the End of a Day' was published by *The Dark Horse* (Scotland) as was 'Jet Lag', the latter commissioned by Sir Arthur Wolfendale for his celebratory volume, *Harrison in the Abbey*, honouring John Harrison, inventor of the Longitude Clock. 'Before Eden' was published by *Poetry Review*; 'Completing the Circle', by *Society Today* (Winter 2006). 'An Even Shorter History of Everything', written to celebrate the installation of Bill Bryson as Chancellor of Durham University on 9 November 2005, appeared in *Other Poetry* (Winter 2006). 'City Lights' was published by the *TLS* in December 2006.

The three dedicatory poems were written to celebrate the 70th birthdays of the poet-dedicatees. 'An Ode on the Changes to be Reckoned with in the New Scotland', for Stewart Conn, was published in *There's a Poem to be Made*, edited by Christine De Luca (Shore Poets, Edinburgh, 2006). 'Listen to the Words', for John Lucas, appeared in *Speaking English*, edited by Andy Croft (Smokestack Books, 2007). 'Metaphors Accepted', for Michael Standen, appeared in *Still Standen*, a special issue of *Other Poetry* edited by James Roderick Burns (July 2007).

*The Myth of Medea* was written in 2003-04 (and revised in summer 2006) as a libretto for a short opera. It appears in this book in a rather more extended form as 'an entertainment'. The Nurse's opening "aria" and the concluding "duet" are quoted from D.W. Lucas's translation of Euripides' *Medea* (Cohen & West, London, 1949).

# CONTENTS

## Prelude

In a summer season, when soft was the sun,
I clad myself crudely in stuff that shepherds wear,
And like a hermit habited, unholy in his ways,
Went wide into this world, wonders to hear.
But on a May morning on Malvern hills,
A marvel befell me, full of magic, I thought:
I was weary for wandering and went me to rest
Under a broad bank by a brawling burn,
And as I lay and leaned and looked at the water,
I slipped into slumber, so merrily it swirled.
Then came a dream to me, marvellously dreamed.
I was in a wilderness, I knew not where,
And behold to the East, set high in the sun,
A tower on a hill-top, beautifully built.
A deep dale lay beneath, a dungeon therein,
Flanked by dark ditches, dreadful to see.
A fair field full of folk I found there between,
Where all manner of men, the mean and the rich,
Were working and wandering, as the world requires.

WILLIAM LANGLAND, *Piers Plowman*,
Prologue, Lines 1-19 (B text)

# A LAMENT FOR THE MAKERS

# A Lament for the Makers

*(to the Memory of Philip Hobsbaum)*

> *I se that makaris amang the laif*
> *Playis heir ther pageant, sine gois to graif;*
> *Sparit is nocht ther faculte;*
> *Timor mortis conturbat me.*
>
> WILLIAM DUNBAR, *c.*1500


## PART ONE

### I

Unsatisfied by summer,
memory hardly anticipates
the darkening year.

But now it's here,
the season of deciduous souls,
gold smouldering to umber

when the sun illuminates
briefly that reredos of beeches
with Byzantine fire.

A last, late finger of grace
still brightens far reaches
of a barbarous empire

lyrically and lovingly.
Most of what we write
time will erase.


### II

Try to remember
how the weather of before
emancipated the leaves.

'O wild west wind' is layered
thick with voices.
*How the sick leaves reel down in throngs.*

11

*In wrothe winde leves*
*Laucen fro the linde*
*And lighten on the grounde.*

*De ramis cadunt folia*
*nam viror totus periit,*
*iam calor liquid omni...*

The same and more.
Most of what our bones know
has been said before.

### III
What is poetry but passion
in immutable form. Ah, love,
its avalanche,

agon and exhilaration
slipping off the tongue
into memory!

Copulation is common
to dragonfly and human,
but memory is sacred

in the underworld of words.
'I have a dream,' said Berryman,
'that the Chambers of the End

will resound with the voices
of poets talking;
a café where Cal & Dylan

disport themselves
in spirit-colloquy
with Yeats and Chaucer.

Milton, the seer, paces
the smooth college lawns
in company with Blake,

while, huge on the horizon,
Homer, forsaken Titan,
strides alone across the asphodels.

And there I shall
at last importune Shakespeare
with my cruxes and queries...'

IV

So, Mr Bones,
what are you crying for?
Who's rattling the murky

Cimmerian door
on both sides of the fable?
Won't you rise, drink blood

and tell us how long
time lasts
in the music of utterance?

If it's blood
you have to have,
you hammering ghosts,

it's your still articulate
breath we crave
who are alive.

V

By the water's edge
Eurydice is leading Orpheus
into the pit,

slipping joyfully through
the cobwebs
in her sparkling dress.

Now they will be together
forever. Why didn't they
think of this before?

Blinded by fog,
he forces the baize,
then the black door.

Out, buzzing like maniacs,
swarm the flies
from their bed of maggots.


## VI

'Follow the tapering root!'
Who spoke?
A resonance, ivy-choked,

from a cellar, once a house,
home to a flourishing oak
and Peter Redgrove, poet,

easing himself through the dust
as if he'd climbed
from the coal seams.

I looked in amazement
at the rainbow
circling his bald head,

then felt myself dissolve
and filter through
an all-surrounding screen

into his dream. What was that
crowd of pearl-grey faces
gathered by the river?

Half in chiaroscuro,
in slow parade, they drifted
beside the peat-black water,

cloudy reflections
shimmering unassailable
in time's aquifer.

'Who are these shades?' I whispered
to the great head
domed beside me that seemed

to have put on visibility
to guide me.
'The scene you see,'

he answered, smiling,
'is the *numen numenorum*,
foundry of dreams.

You can, if you fancy,
call this swamp, Acheron,
this river, Lethe,

and those spectres massed
in mist along its bank,
souls, once poets,

who have not yet
earned a guilt-free
passage to oblivion.

Life after death,
you see, is nothing like
what we expected.

Earth's unrecorded guests,
lacking the moon's gift,
slip from the noose of their names

straight through the river
into the animal bliss
of forgetting.

Such is the infinite mercy
of our blind mother.
Her gift? Mutability, delivered

alike to every link in the chain
of birth's formation
and dying's transformation.

For in death, the enduring energies
hired for life
to work in our self-factories

take themselves off into fresh things:
sperm, embryos, mayflies,
maggots, millipedes, moth-codlings.

Only we who insistently
insinuate ourselves
through art into memory

are condemned to linger
for a time in Limbo,
hovering on the left bank of Lethe,

where, as you see, we inhabit
the versions of ourselves
that you devise and call our reputations.'

As the poet finished speaking,
a blood tint rouged the mist
that massed around him.

Then the crowd suddenly rose –
a blizzard of insects,
so many I could not believe

fame had undone so many,
blinding me,
battering my hair and mouth.

I lay in an agony
of just-woken tears,
accepting those stings like kisses.

## PART TWO

### I

A dream? No, more
A writhing sea of dreams
that tossed me to the shore

only to claw me back
and fill my eyes,
wide open, as before,

with that same haunted plain,
empty now, and flat,
though everywhere pitted, it seemed,

with little round pools,
each with a sheen
like linen laid across it.

'News? Have you news for me?'
A tarn by my feet,
a steaming puddle, seemed to speak.

Kneeling, I searched its surface
for a face,
finding at first my own

masked by a swirl of scum
that like a necklace
circled, twisting to become

a frame for her whose features,
lovely in life, had been
to Dis, so irresistible

that, slumped in the torpor of his myth,
he roused himself
disguised as cells of cancer

to rake her from the earth.
'Frances! I want you, Frances,'
he whispered in her ear.

And she, terrified, resisting,
had to succumb.
Now, like water crowfoot flowing,

she opened her arms,
but as they rose to mine,
my hands slipped through them,

emerging moist with mist,
feeling no flesh,
while a soft, mute exhalation

fanned my fingers.
'Could I believe' –
an echo sighing –'that you're alive,

I'd know for certain
that the living and dead
inhabit one house under the sky.

But news, please, news
of Adam, my son,
who must, in time, be a man.'

'Adam is well,' I answered,
'a man, a poet,
one foot set in childhood, where

you're still woven through him;
the other, unfixed,
unsure in a world still brutal

to the vulnerable and gentle.'
Faintly a soft, 'I knew it'
circled outward like a ripple

from those half relinquished lips.
Then, 'To meet him here
is what I least would wish.

For as he was,
I have him boyish with me always.
As he is, he'd be more

strange to me
than I am to the feeling self I was
when I was flesh.

For this is the price of salvation:
to lose... not sight,
but all happiness of the skin.

Touch that was ecstasy
to my breast, and, oh,
to the soft mouth of my womb...

Touch that hallowed for me even
the rack of childbirth...
I would die again for the pain of it!'

She spoke, breaking with a cry
into a watery mosaic.
I watched her ebb away

into what seemed suddenly
to be an estuary
on fire with burning fountains.

## II

'Hot springs.' A voice at my elbow.
'Sulphur?' 'Who knows?'
'Vortices of magma. Hell stuff!'

A man's voice. A woman's.
'Come on Ted!
We're going to miss the reading!'

Three? Or three in one?
A sort of three-fold bubble
hung trembling at the mouth

of a red plastic wand
through which a child's breath
fanned them –

a bright one, a dark one,
and in between,
the man in black feathers

who zoomed into close-up
crying 'You!'
Then hesitated.

'Yes,' I parried,
'But never one of those
your spirit hated.

As you see,
I don't belong here.
Nor do I expect her

who despaired of life when love
abandoned her
to recognise her biographer.'

'Enough of that.'
He groaned as he
struggled to shake himself

free of the hands that clutched him –
the painted fingernails
he lurched between.

'Will nothing I wrote
deliver me
from my fate as scapegoat?

Say I deserve it!
Say I wagered my will
against theirs, and lost the bet.

It is fair, I ask you,
to be forever
framed in punishment?

A look of pity was
all my answer,
but he shook it off.

'If only they would know me
as I was,
as I laid myself open in poetry.

What I miss
is the redbreast's crooked twitter
and the wren's cry

piercing the hedgerow
early in April;
primroses at shoe-level

repeating their clockwork miracle;
wheel ruts and
rain pools quick with frog-spawn,

while lurking in the tea-brown river,
the sleek trout
dart or dawdle under willow spray

fresh sapped for king fisher
and Fisher King
before the swallows return.'

He turned away,
throbbing, at the heart
of his own tear,

stumbling back to rejoin
that trinity
of sad, inseparable souls

precisely at the moment
another broke away
and bowled towards me,

meaning, I thought, to greet me.
But no, like an X ray,
she passed through me.

'You are amazed,'
it was Redgrove's voice,
'But for Sylvia you don't exist,

having no place in her past.
She is here,
in part, because of you,

in the mirror and bubble
of your book,
but don't expect a look

of recognition. To her
you're invisible,
a shade more insubstantial

than she, to you.
The dreams of the dead
don't feature unknown faces.'

'But if the dead dream,' I said,
'isn't the afterlife, after all
time's solvent?

Isn't Shakespeare
your eternal contemporary,
with Dante, Pushkin, Marvell?

Is there no shared fountain
of the living word
where timelessly the poets gather?'

'Philosophy's to blame' –
a woman's voice, American –
'for giving poets such an awful name.

Since Plato banished us
for cheating truth for fame,
the official keepers of ideas,

not gods, but all too human,
have allotted each of us
a glittering prison.

We're labelled according to
when we wrote
and what we thought was true.

Look! Every patine of bright gold
(Shakespeare toying with Pythagoras)
that you, in ignorance, behold

in the heaven-field spread about you,
is a creator's soul
sealed in an academic cell,

cut off by some proliferating theory
from its source – its loves,
its learning, its redeeming thread

of curiosity and doubt;
even from the corners of childhood.
For a buried childhood

can become an open grave,
an archive thumbed
by every sycophant PhD alive.'


III

The young married woman sits at her
battered Smith Corona
typing a letter to Miss Bishop.

'Dear Elizabeth, I do so admire...'
Somewhere behind her,
a curtain catches fire.

Finishing the letter becomes urgent
as flames consume
the window frame, the carpet.

Now the desk is ablaze.
Should she move into the bedroom?
Or did the fire start there?

'Jump from the balcony!'
A low voice, thick
with humorous contempt. Whose?

I'm desperate to remember...
wondering as I wake,
whatever became of that typewriter?

Who am I for whom another day
shatters a nightmare?
I open the morning a little way,

grieving, half asleep, for
all the thoroughbred typewriters
put out to grass

by writers whose racing fingers
they used to obey.
What digital itch trapped progress

in a virtual web where
language insists,
kilobyte after kilobyte,

on being writ on air
everywhere and nowhere?
What network exists

that will carry electronic
language-bundles
into Avernus?

I pace between shelves
of recorded voices
stacked like skulls

ready to speak to me
when I play them,
ready to wear their faces,

though they can neither see
nor hear me,
these ghosts in the machine.

Does communion only occur
according to custom
in the hinterland of dream?

I hear, like rain, the genii loci
of beloved places,
revoking the laws of time,

keeping safe the never retrievable
from the gulled masses
in a shameful England up for sale.

Where is the Wessex
Thomas Hardy loved? Where
Clare's wide, untrafficked Essex?

IV

'Words, words, words' –
echoes fading in the ear
as a gentle revenant appeared

I knew for Edward Thomas
by his look of patient,
undisguised despair.

'Well, England must be ugly now.
I died in good time,
escaping the finale of her dotage.

Hers was a world half ruined
when I went to war.
I see her struggling to renew herself,

careless of her image,
slipshod, rich and ignorant
from contaminated soil. And yet,

there must be some who care,
a few who tend her garden
in the wild places, still.

Without me, no doubt,
summer is in spate again,
flowering over England and Wales.

Time's wheel will still be turning
on the axle of its arrow.
The redstarts will be back from Africa,

breeding among the crab apples.
Foxgloves must be burning
up the long wire of their stems.

Lovely, head-high unclaimed grasses –
I see them lucent and astir,
each one tasselled according to its kind.'

V

'Nostalgia, the poet's pitfall!'
(That unmistakable Welsh lilt.)
'I drowned my grief in alcohol,

nightly dissolving my days.
Whisky jerry-built
walkways over the quicksands,

Whisky and the weather of whisky,
smoother of worry ways.
All that booze and boisterousness

backed up to accuse me,
but I wrote the poems, didn't I?
The music was in me.

Oh, I took my muse with me.
Dragged the bitch
from her bar stool, a pouting doxy

inherited from Marlowe, maybe,
time-shared with
MacDiarmid and Louis.

Not a nice nurse, no-o-o, a right whore!
And you aim to woo her
with workshops and herbal tea?

Listen, ladies, poetry's no cure.
She's a killer! And she chose me.
The unchosen never get near her.'

*

Fading off. Then fainter,
low but near,
there rose a bleaker shade.

'I didn't think
I still could be afraid,
I'd settled that

God's vast,
*moth-eaten musical brocade*
would leave me flat.

A fly, fly-swatted on
high window glass
gives up and dies there.

I looked for endless
deep blue air
that is nothing and nowhere,

not planning, as you know
to take a bow
from the fun-house mirrors

of posterity's freak show.
When I dreamed up
Balokowsky and his kind,

I only joked that I'd be
mince meat
in the academic grind.

But Jake is all too real,
His undertow
keeps dragging me down

to how I used to feel
when I was low.
I'm bait he dangles for his PhD.

And, Christ, what's worse
is I invented me,
I said it first!

Jake's just an imitator
missing the poignant irony
of his creator.

I was a romantic topiary,
really, cut to shape
by shears I couldn't see

but felt clip-clipping round me
as a child.
My heart was Yeatsian,

sensuous, driven wild
by thoughts I knew
I never could escape.

Love stood begging for me
with an empty cup.
Owlish, shy – yes, odd,

I half anticipated
they'd not let me grow up,
the ones I hated.

That's what you get (says God?)
for being such a
whingeing, miserable old sod.

Perhaps. But before you slick,
prize-toting new guys
write me off,

take it from me I didn't
whine so much
as watch the levelling approach

of poetry's demise.
I can't believe the future,
now, has any time for verse.

The hopeless media scum
today, of course,
will still be hot for 'culture',

but my guess is it won't be long
before the girls
are wearing tee shirts scrawled with

*Bring Back Patience Strong!*

### VI

What was that? A rumble of storm
like gun fire:

*In the beginning was the Word.*
The voice of Milton
caught by Miłosz?

'I survived by incantation,
heard my own words
waken as my lips perished.

My mind raced blindfold,
through the interstellar night.
When my eyes eased open,

I saw the door,
and crawled under its lintel
into the light...'

*O dark, dark, dark*
*They all go into the dark,*
*The vacant interstellar spaces...*

How was it that I heard,
yet couldn't join
that all-male choir of voices?

*One raft on the veiled*
*flood of Acheron,*
*Marius and Jugurtha together...*

Lowell and Berryman together,
Frost and Sandburg,
Muir and MacDiarmid.

*One tangle of shadows,*
*when, when and whenever*
*death closes our eyelids.*

And then the clouds peeled off.
I watched them roll away
like dream fluff –

so many bruised, tempestuous souls
transformed in the light of morning,
into a golden fleece.

### VII

So, on which tangle of hopes,
in whose memory
shall I reverently place a wreath?

On MacCaig's or Bunting's,
Silkin's or Donaghy's,
Bill Scammell's? Ric Caddel's?

There are quite enough
poets in hell,
quite enough excellent poets.

Miss Moore, Miss Millay.
Miss Beer, Miss Bishop.
Anne Ridler of deep belief.

*And he's at last tane in his maw*
*Gud Gael Turnbull, loved by aw,*
*Great reuth it we that so should be.*

And which of us in our dire
concupiscence today
for equal acclaim and power

will the future honour
with Euterpe's lyre,
once we are ash and clay?

'You will be saved,' cries Art,
'by creative writing!'
'Not so,' says Experience.

'When conscience and feeling
castrated the Classics,
Christ introduced his appealing

promise of another life;
but like all metaphysical tactics,
that meant teaching

the spirit to endure the flesh –
then let it go;
let it unravel at the right tempo.'

*When the daughters of music*
*shall be brought low,*
*and the grasshopper shall be a burden,*

*and desire shall fail*
*because man goeth to his long home* –
I will lay down my book.

To the making of books
there will be an end;
and to their makers, also.

To the makers of love?
Even that goddess is mortal,
whether or not it's true

that *love, love, love,*
*is the only green in the jungle.*
What can we do?

Before the beginning – unknown.
As after the end – unknown.
But floating, stretched between,

the mind's harmonic mappings,
frail as gossamer,
*costing not less than everything.*

I am alive. I'm human.
Get dressed. Make coffee.
Shore a few lines against my ruin.

# STONE MILK

# Near the End of a Day

Was that a butterfly
fluttering down to the grass
or a dead leaf?
A leaf, a leaf.
I can't see anywhere
the corpse of a butterfly.

Is that a white feather
asleep on the terrace,
or white cat's fur?
A feather, a feather
with a tiny grey caterpillar
curled at its root.

It is with such
questions and answers
near the end of a day
near the end of a summer
near the end of my life
that I reassure myself.

# Stone Milk
*Sils-Maria, Graubunden, 2006*

A backward May, with all the local finches of the Fex Tal
        piping in dialect.
'Gruezi' to the nun-white finger-high crocuses
        thinly nursing to life the flattened fields.
'Gruezi' to the fisted bristles colouring the larches
        a green to break your heart.
The fairytale resorts, scrubbed clean but closed
        because the coach crowds haven't arrived yet,
look to be hospitals for convalescent ideals.

Imagine a breath held long before history happened,
allowing a lake to drown its Jurassic numbness
        in Elysian blue.
Conceive of the gentians' daytime midnight 'smoking
        torch-like out of Pluto's gloom',
Eden's anemones lifting from pale Blakean nightgowns
        faces of incorruptible innocence.
If stones could be milked, these fleeting rivers of melt
        would feed us like flowering trees,
since Mother Earth, you say, after eons of glacial childbirth
        brings up her whole brood naturally.

But naturally what I want and need and expect is to be loved.
So why, as I grow older, when I lift up my eyes to the hills –
        raw deserts that they are –
do they comfort me (not always but sometimes)
        with the pristine beauty of my almost absence?
Not the milk of kindness, but the milk of stones
        is food I'm learning to long for.

# Before Eden
*(for Paul Stangroom)*


A day opens, a day closes,
Each day like every other day.
No day is like another day.

A wave crashes, a wave caresses,
Each wave like the next wave.
None sweeps the same arc on the sand.

A wall fits its belt to a hill
As a mason fits stone to hand.
No stone's like any other stone,

And every stone has a like stone.
Why should another spring surprise me?
The gorse still erupts from the scrubland,

The gulls again screech to the landfill.
What claims identity
That isn't self-propelled, vicious, multiple, alone?

Think of how it was before Eden.
God held his breath,
The fresh-moulded clay in his hands,

Hesitating between dream and achievement.
The mountains were there,
Fixed in a clear, viscous element

He would need to exchange for air.
Trees flowered, gorgeous as palaces,
All without fruit, without rot,

Had bacteria and seeds been invented?
Yes, but they didn't have uses.
The birds and creatures were there,

Evolved already in his mind,
Lifelessly waiting while
The pivotal question tormented him:

What sort of nature did he want?
Once he'd breathed life into Adam,
He knew he couldn't take it back!

He himself might have to be
Re-created, risking
His hand-crafted system, risking death.

No life without birth.
No growth without waste.
No first step without a last.

It was such perfect weather,
That sparkling morning of the sixth day
When God, in his pride, looked over

His hard week's work, saw that it was good.
And hesitated.
If the sky had admitted one cloud,

If the mountains had understood
The whispering ice,
Or loved the molten nature of being,

If a bird had cried out, or if
A locust had filleted sound,
Or if terror had *said*...

He might have thought the fifth day would suffice.
But the *Gipfeln* nursing the rhododendrons,
Even the Tree of Knowledge, said nothing.

It was silence that broke him in the end.
With every perfect day identical,
No animating evil could arise.

So God bent down and sighed the words,
'I will.'
He spoke, and Adam opened all his eyes.

# The Enigma

Falling to sleep last night in a deep crevasse
between one rough dream and another, I seemed,
still awake, to be stranded on a stony path,
and there the familiar enigma presented itself
in the shape of a little trembling lamb.
It was lying like a pearl in the trough between
one Welsh slab and another, and it was crying.

I looked around, as anyone would, for its mother.
Nothing was there. What did I know about lambs?
Should I pick it up? Carry it...where?
What would I do if it were dying? The hand
of my conscience fought with the claw of my fear.
It wasn't so easy to imitate the Good Shepherd
in that faded, framed Sunday School picture
filtering now through the dream's daguerreotype.

With the wind fallen and the moon swollen to the full,
small, white doubles of the creature at my feet
flared like candles in the creases of the night
until it looked to be alive with new born lambs.
Where could they all have come from?
A second look, and the bleating lambs were birds –
kittiwakes nesting, clustered on a cliff face,
fixing on me their dark accusing eyes.

There was a kind of imperative not to touch them,
yet to be of them, whatever they were –
now lambs, now birds, now floating points of light –
fireflies signalling how many lost New England summers?
One form, now another; one configuration, now another.
Like fossils locked deep in the folds of my brain,
outliving a time by telling its story. Like stars.

# Completing the Circle *

*(i.m. Anita Jackson who feared her work had come to nothing)*

Two panels of glass
stretched one above the other,
two panes of blue glass...

Kandinsky, Bach at the organ
tossing sunlight between
voices, some whole, some broken.

The mathematics of colour sings
brave as a rainbow
that rubs itself out against air.

But dying is the water side of waking;
yellow is not all.
You can strike light

out of the bruised seventh
in the Dorian scale,
or out of an imaginary curve

that completes the red circle
of a life's yearning
solely at night, beyond eyesight.


\* 'Death is a side of life that is turned away from us...The true figure of life
extends through both domains, the blood of the mightiest circulation drives
through both: there is neither a here nor a beyond, but a great unity...'

RAINER MARIA RILKE

39

# Waving Goodbye

*(to my son Charles leaving Wales in a strong north westerly)*


Shadows pelt over the hills at a furious gallop;
Cloud-horses form and reform, group and regroup –
Impermanence brushing inscrutable purple and green
On a canvas of morning you'll barely claim;
Nor will you catch me mourning as you drive away,
Away from where we stand in the sunlight waving,
While you wave, too, from the car's bucking window.

So you went, and every thought, vowel and verb
Of what you are went with you;
Every syllable and page of what you will do
Or may say, all your everydays of solitude or multitude,
All the vague, massed cumuli of your intent
Went with you, out of an us, out of an ours,
As the gate clanged shut into a new story. Yours. All yours.

# Orcop

*Remembering Frances Horovitz (1938–1983)*

Driving south from Hereford one day in March
memorable for trickling piles of snow, with sideshows,
drift upon drift of snowdrops lapping the hedgerows,
we sighted the signpost, and on impulse, turned up
the winding, vertical road to Orcop. The church,
further away from the village than I remembered,
was no less an image of you than I remembered,
with its high-pitched, peasant roof and wooden steeple
gracing a slope with yew trees and a painter's view –
ploughed red soil, a pasture, a working barn –
that set it apart from the ordinary, just as your field stone,
when we found it, set you apart from the good people
labelled in polished marble, buried around you.
As in your life, though never aloof, you were alone.
I remembered how, when you quietly entered a room
in one of those woven dresses you used to wear,
heather or lavender, all senseless chattering would cease,
shamed by your dignity. I remembered your beautiful things:
your pots, your books, your cat, silver as your cross,
your delicate drawings. Yes, I remembered you exactly.
And there you were, still – beautiful, exceptional,
in a landscape of lichen I had to read like Braille
to find your name. I heard the first blackbird, then a thrush.
Later, as we left, the children we'd seen playing
among the graves when we arrived resumed their game,
using your stone, a hump from another century,
to hide behind, while one, the smallest, counted slowly.

# Inheriting My Grandmother's Nightmare

Consider the adhesiveness of things
    to the ghosts that prized them,
the 'olden days' of birthday spoons
    and silver napkin rings.
Too carelessly I opened
    that velvet drawer of heirlooms.
There lay my grandmother's soul
begging under veils of tarnish to be brought back whole.

She who was always a climate in herself,
    who refused to vanish
as the nineteen-hundreds grew older and louder
    and the wars worse
and her grandchildren, bigger and ruder
    in her daughter's house.
How completely turned around
her lavender world became, how upside down.

And how much, under her 'flyaway' hair,
    she must have suffered,
sitting there ignored by the dinner guests
    hour after candle-lit hour,
rubbed out, like her initials on the silverware,
    eating little, passing bread,
until the wine's flood, the smoke's blast,
the thunderous guffaws at last roared her to bed.

In her tiny garden of confidence,
    wasted she felt, and furious.
She fled to church, but Baby Jesus
    had outgrown his manger.
She read of Jews in *The New Haven Register*
    gassed or buried alive.
Every night, at the wheel of an ambulance,
she drove and drove, not knowing how to drive.

She died in '55, paralysed, helpless.
Her no-man's-land survived.
I light my own age with a spill
from her distress. And there it is,
her dream, my heirloom, my drive downhill
at the wheel of the last bus,
the siren's wail, the smoke, the sickly smell.
The drawer won't shut again. It never will.

# An Even Shorter History of Nearly Everything
*(for Bill Bryson)*


Should you find yourself today on the road to Newcastle,
You couldn't miss, nailed to the horizon,
The armed wings of the north's super-angel
Smelted from the embers of its past.
Part phoenix, part satellite, part Lucifer,
Faceless and sexless, it embodies vast
Crowds of miniature working people
Welded into an elevated whole,
As if to cancel evolutionary nature
And replace it with a single global soul.

The Angel electronically stores the dead,
Communicates by radar, commands
Through a computer in its head.
You'll notice that it has dispensed with hands,
So never could have built this stone cathedral
Whose shoulders, a short nine hundred years ago,
Shoved aside the coal seams and still stands,
A Rock of Ages in the evening glow,
Shrugging off raids by pylon and power cable –
Our world the hands that raised it couldn't know

Any more than they could know the local stones
They shaped with mathematical exactness
For luminous Cuthbert and Bede's stolen bones
Were seas squeezed solid long before man's genesis,
Were relics, world upon world, beneath a crust
They reckoned sixty centuries in the making –
Thin as a tissue dropped on Everest,
But packed like New York with nearly everything
That translates time into language for us.
We need to name the images we trust.

How is it that, alone among breeding creatures,
We feel compelled to create for ourselves,
Again and again in the image of ourselves,
A sacred exoskeleton, claiming for ourselves
Powers to preserve our uniqueness? Not as we are,
But as shells leave signs in the sand:
Relics of Christian worship, Christian war,
Reminders that 'in our beginning is our end',
Heaps of DNA in cryptic rooms,
The Nevilles hacked to pieces on their tombs,

News that this palace, theatre, fortress, prison
Was achieved by some genius of the pointed arch
Who read his Bible but couldn't read the rocks
Dragged from the Carboniferous to frill a church
With storms of fossils, individual as snowflakes
Three hundred million years adrift with the continents,
Locked in the ooze of an equatorial ocean.
What faith, what story, what fact is more remarkable
Than this resurrection of the dead that represents
The life in us, the strangeness of it all?

*The fossil-decorated black pillars to be found in Durham Cathedral
were made from polished shafts of crystallised limestone known as
Frosterley Marble. County Durham's great limestone strata was once
a shallow seabed of free-swimming corals that over three hundred million years
ago thronged the equatorial oceans of the Lower Carboniferous.*

# Jet Lag

*Time is to clock as mind is to brain.*
DAVA SOBEL
in *Longitude*

Most of the time my age fits me exactly;
The clock on my wrist keeps time
        with the clock inside me;
The seconds pile up minutely into days,
Thickening into wrinkles of Sundays and Mondays,
        sunny days, moony days –
So time passes within me and through me,
Conveying me on its slow-moving walkway
Out of the duty-free clap trap of the airport
Into a desert of a new dimension
        where it ionises and splits up.

If, from my choice meridian, I decide to fly
Westward through the lines of longitude,
I'll spring into New York or Boston
        five hours younger;
If eastward to Islamabad or Almaty, I'll arrive
Sleepless, in a grouchy mood, five hours older.
Meantime, my ticking pulse will punish me
        for being alive,
For keeping my home time going like Harrison's clock,
Mechanical, reliable, but in life's time, unpredictable,
        like sailor's luck.

## City Lights

*Apocalypse London. Burning again in glass,*
*Call it Sleaze Street, Croesus' carnival. The Word made steel...*
as I stumble from some urinous underpass,
pulled up suddenly by the great conch of St. Paul
cast like a fossil or a shelled moon on the clay-white
phosphorescent shore The City calls night,
revealed in its splash of glory
as a vessel of arrested, accepted, outwardly reflected light
beamed from a long way off – like the Christian story,
while Babylon burns from within – like Satan's sin.

# Beach Kites

Is this a new way of being born?
To feel some huge crescent personality
burgeoning out of your shoulders,
winging you over the sand, the sluggish sea?
Mile upon mile of contaminated Wash is
tucking a cold March sky into the horizon.

You can drive no further.
Look down at the thrashing water,
the upfalls of its reach
failing, failing again to take the cliff –
sandpipers hunch on the geomorphic ledge –
rock face and wave force, story without speech.

But it's one thing to pause at the cutting edge,
another to face the evolving beach, the gap
where the road stops and the dunes heap
and the wind blows fiercely in the wrong direction.

One gaudy comma ascends... another... another...
the air is rocking alert with punctuation.

Grey sickle cells cluster under a microscope.

A jumbo wasp, a pterodactyl, a peacock feather
jockey for space against moon-parings, rainbow zeppelins,
prayer flags – imagination battling with imagination,
spotted species chasing the plain – as out they float,
strong men steering their wild umbilical toys

away from the girlfriends in the car park, who
leathered from heel to neck in steel-studded black,
headscarfed against the wind, seem coolly resigned
to an old dispensation, a ritual of mating
that puts up again with the cliff-hanging habits of boys.
Is this a new way of writing?
The heroes off flying or fighting, the women waiting?

# The Blackbird at Pwllymarch

*(for Stephen Regan)*

Because I live here
I have learned from the gorsebush
how to whistle yellow petals
out of my bright beak,

though I can remember
wooded fells loud with waterfalls
and curlews crying in the marsh
that was once a lake.

*After the 9th century Irish lyric,*
*'The Blackbird at Belfast Lough'*

# THREE DEDICATIONS

## An Ode on the Changes to be Reckoned with in the New Scotland
*(for Stewart Conn at 70)*


A pint with a whisky was called a 'nip & chaser',
As if nips could be chaste by the time they got inside.
My mind paints a huddle of sleeves on a puddled counter,
Drams like pert wee wifies standing beside.
Looking back through the fug & reek & pints of laughter,
I can just about make out the poets, ranked in their pride,
Rumbling and preening like spurred cocks cooped together.

For those were the last of the Grieved years, so to speak,
When makers made verses, & lassies queued to be made.
One evening the sainted MacDiarmid pecked my cheek.
I covered the sanctified spot with a band-aid
And swore I wouldn't wash it for a week.
Halcyon days! Gone with the wit, I'm afraid.
Caledonia's frivolous Muse is past her peak.

The poets she favoured are dead, or else can't drink.
And look how the pesticide Virtue's scoured the land!
Ye cannae smoke. Ye cannae flirt. Ye cannae blink
Without some officious official cawing 'banned!'
Scotland's white rose is plastic, bubble-gum pink.
A sober man kicks at the thistle pricking his hand.
What would MacCaig, what would Garioch think?

Well, what they never did know can't hurt them now.
It's time the girls had a go on the golden lyre.
They won't, 'when pain and anguish wring the brow',
Be ministering angels, and they'll never again inspire
Immortal song. But drink up, gentlemen, anyhow!
The old arrow's dipped in a fresh new brew of desire,
And love is a scratch even Virtue will have to allow.

# Listen to the Words

*A 'fully interactive poetry experience' for John Lucas at 70*


'I-pod' is a hideous word,
While 'mobile phone', although euphonious,
Chirps from its ambulant nest like a digital bird.
As for the razz-ma-tazzda of TESCO and ASDA,
For an epithet that doesn't sound erroneous
Why not try on ACRONYMONIOUS?

Precisely what does 'interactive' mean?
Just being friendly? Or something more obscene?
Should I 'download' the messages I'm 'text'd'?
Is making love the same as 'having sex'?
The verb 'to party' isn't quite the same
As putting your manners on and *going* to one.
No, 'partying' is an 'innovative' game
Like virtual food, or vandals having fun.

'To be honest' and speak my mind,
Dear John, my guess is that 'at this point in time'
English is leaving you and me behind.
Do you know how to teach a sound to bite?
Do I go surfing through a net all night?
Lacking 'promotional strategies', I'm afraid
We'll hardly make the canon's hit parade.

Still, appearing 'live' at seventy has
A tingling, clear, unsponsored compensation.
Like fugue motifs in Bach, like flowering jazz,
Those plummet lines of language, free of fashion,
Reach to your deepest layer and won't let go.
There, every minute tells you lightly, gently,
*The still sad music of humanity*
Is all we know, and all we need to know.

## Metaphors Accepted *or*

### *The History of Things Would Always Be Getting Lost*
### *If It Weren't for Writers like Michael Standen*

When he looked back over the wet lawn
to the sepia school of childhood,
it was like being a hollowed-out turnip
peering from the inside of its smile.
Memory, knitting patterns in the dark,
purled a fine wind of betrayal into the air.
And he was where?

Beached on the blue hem of England,
a shy boy inspecting life in a time-pool,
spying on uncles, looking for love clues,
stumbling over stories smoothed and smoothed again
by the repetitious action of his pen.

Each day he watched his world inch down
the same shrivelling wick of the sun
to rekindle itself in the same indignant ash,
the same ember-dramas of helplessness and learning
heaped up behind huge flaming wars.
So he wrote of what he couldn't help but notice
as the lion's skin slipped off the back
of the Empire's Man of Destiny,
reverting, on his own (coalless) hearth, to a hearth rug.

On which, crossed legged, he sits, this man of poetry,
this gift of Egypt, still conducting, from his magic carpet,
the workings of his own special launderette;
still able, after decades of washing and spin-drying
the itchy rags of England's worn out conscience,
to lift off cleanly from new landing grounds,
raising up our exhausted condition –
phoney art, easy sex and sick health care –
against the gravity of the situation and unhelpful air.

*Most of the images in this poem are Michael Standen's,*
*unabashedly filched in celebration of his stories and poems.*

# THE MYTH OF MEDEA

*An Entertainment*

# CAST:

EURIPIDES
MEDEA
JASON
CREON/AEGEUS
CHORUS: Medea's old NURSE
        A young wife
        A middle-aged housewife
Dancers, Musicians, as in a Greek Tragedy.

# OVERTURE

*As the curtain rises, the entire cast, wearing jeans and T-shirts, is putting the finishing touches to the set of a classical Greek city.* CREON *comes forward with a black (or white) board on which has been written in coloured chalk,* THE MYTH OF MEDEA. *The* NURSE *contemplates this for a minute, then corrects the title to* THE OFFICIAL MYTH OF MEDEA. *Seeing this,* EURIPIDES *angrily cleans the board with a rag and scrawls in large letters,* THE MEDEA BY EURIPIDES. *The set finished, the actors approach a large costume box, stage left, and take from it scarves and robes, all vaguely Greek in character, which they put on over their jeans. Finally* EURIPIDES *removes a pile of scripts from the box and calls the cast together.*

## SCENE I

EURIPIDES. Everybody here? Good, good. (*He passes out scripts which should be pocketed as the play proceeds.*) Jason, Creon, Nurse, Chorus 1, Chorus 2. And Medea. You should know your parts by now, but you'll notice I've made one or two concessions to your feelings. If you have further objections, of course, I'm open to suggestion. Now, let's begin. Nurse, Chorus, take your places please.

*The* NURSE *comes forward for her opening aria. The rest of the cast remains on stage, out of the spotlight.*

NURSE. Oh, that the Argo had never slipped through the Clashing Rocks,
To beach at Colchis, that Pelion's virgin pines
Had never been hacked down for oars!
Then would Medea be a mighty queen in Colchis,
Not powerless in Corinth, weakened by marriage to Jason.

MEDEA. (*Interrupting.*) No, I still don't like the way this story begins. Weak? I? Directly descended from the Sun?

EURIPIDES. Well, then, how do you propose to open the show?

MEDEA. From the very first line
I mean to voice my point of view.
(*To the* CHORUS.)
Let me put it to you ladies. What comes to mind
When you hear the name, Medea? Tell me.
Be frank. Forget about politeness.
Don't you think of murder?

Don't you think of a woman criminal by nature,
Schooled in witchcraft, worse than Lady Macbeth?
A wife so mad with jealousy, she put her sons to death?

CHORUS. No. Yes. No. Yes.

1ST CHORUS. (*Miffed.*) I have a very small part in your drama.

2ND CHORUS. (*Sympathetic.*) It's not your fault, Medea.
Murdering is what you do.

MEDEA. Bull! I thought you were my friends!
Don't you see that every ugly thing you've heard about me –
My every wicked deed, so called, and treachery –
All, all are inventions of ambitious men?
Men like Euripides and Jason – who are terrified of women!
(EURIPIDES *attempts to intervene.*)
No, don't interrupt until you've heard me out!
What woman, what wife, what mother would ever do
What your misogynous mind tells me to?

EURIPIDES. Dear lady, you haven't read me.
Twenty-four centuries of scholarship confirm
My reputation for sympathy with women.
(*To the* CHORUS.) She's crazy!

MEDEA. No, Euripides, I'm strong and bitter,
Fed up to the teeth with your lying slander!
After twenty-four centuries of being misunderstood,
I'd like to explain to this up-to-date audience
Why my reputation as a murderess is undeserved!

(*She reaches for a snapshot in her jeans pocket under her robe and
shows it proudly around to the cast.*)

Look, here are my boys, fit as fiddles both of them.
Would a doting mother murder lads like these?

That I contrived the permanent disappearance of Pelias,
I won't deny – but consider, Jason!
He usurped your father's throne. He deserved to be soup.
As for killing my brother, stuff and nonsense!
The kid fell overboard...

EURIPIDES. All this has nothing to do with my play, in which
My sympathies rest entirely with you, Medea.
You're the diva! I've given you the best lines.

JASON.  For heaven's sake, Medea, let's get on with the performance!
Where exactly do you want to begin?

MEDEA.  With my heart-rending song of betrayal, page 4.
Let's cut straight to there.

EURIPIDES.  And omit three whole pages of my poetry?
If you knew how long it takes to write one line!

MEDEA.  If you knew how long my reputation has suffered
From the lies the Corinthians paid you to write about me!
This time The Myth of Medea is going to be *my* story!

MEDEA *marches up to the board and vigorously erases* THE MEDEA
BY EURIPIDES, *writing on it instead,* THE MEDEA BY MEDEA.
EURIPIDES, *in despair, joins* JASON *and* CREON *to one side, where
they confer conspiratorially. Meanwhile,* MEDEA, *drawing the chorus
around her, launches into her aria.*

MEDEA.  The pain. The pain. I cannot bear the pain.
What wife, deserted and betrayed, could bear such pain?
O faithful Artemis, sister Hecate, let me die!
Send me, father Helios, a crown of fire
Lit from the furnace of my blood and brain.
Lap me in flames. Scorch my body dry.
Reduce me to ash, dear gods. Let clouds of anguish
Billow from my pyre.

1ST CHORUS.  O unhappy woman of Colchis.
We know that Jason's left you for another wife.
We share your misery, yet listen to us.
Think of your children before you take your life.

MEDEA.  Better to die than watch my children suffer.
Why should I live?
No agony could stab me in the grave.

NURSE.  You see how she is? And who can blame her?
Jason reneged upon his sacred oath –
Sworn before all the gods – to love forever
The woman who, to rescue him, betrayed herself.

MEDEA. (*With hands outstretched.*)  Women of Corinth.
I come to you, afraid you may find fault with me.
I am a foreigner. My face is dark. That would be
Enough to put most Greeks off completely.
Yet here I am, your neighbour, a woman like you,

A wife, divorced, with nothing left to live for.
I married for love, as many of us do,
Believing in him, despite his low IQ.

CHORUS. Poor lady, how well we understand you!

1ST CHORUS. We have to act stupid, don't we, to prove men strong.

2ND CHORUS. They have to be right, so we are – artfully – wrong.

MEDEA. And not because Nature made them specially clever!
We're taught from birth to make them think they are.
When all goes well, the subtle wife pretends
Nothing her hero-husband does offends.
Ha! Who hasn't heard them roaring in the bar,
*Keep them pregnant and barefoot!* Zeus forgive me,
I'd rather fight three wars than bear one baby.

CHORUS. Ai. Ai. We agree. We're no more to them than
Plumbing primed and pumped to give them children.

1ST CHORUS. But tell us more, Medea. It is true
Your husband has married again?

2ND CHORUS. Can he have left you
Without a word of apology or excuse?

MEDEA. Jason? I knew when I married him, of course,
That he was the slave of ego and ambition.
So yes, he's found himself a ripe, fragrant plum,
A princess, no less, old King Creon's daughter,
Juicy at sixteen, with little pert breasts
And that red, pouting mouth every pretty girl flaunts
Before she marries and learns what's coming to her.

EURIPIDES. (*Interrupting.*) That vicious piece of sleaze
Is not in my script. Cut it, please!

MEDEA. Jealous I may be, but never disrespectful of women.
You didn't even give her a name!

EURIPIDES.            I didn't know her name.

MEDEA. Well, I do. Glauke.

EURIPIDES.            What's your source?

MEDEA. Robert Graves, if you must know.

EURIPIDES.            An unreliable, latter-day Romantic.

MEDEA. Stick to your verses, Euripides. Leave women to me.
Who but a chauvinist would think up lines like these?
'We women are afraid to hold a sword,
So timid we are, and helpless!'
Just the kind of type-casting I object to!

CREON. (*Bumbling forward.*) Sorry, I seem to have missed my cue.
(*Assuming a kingly posture.*)
Medea. I fear you are resentful of your husband.

MEDEA. (*Bitterly.*) My former husband!

CREON.                              Ah. So you accept the status quo.

MEDEA. (*Falling to her knees.*) Creon, I grovel before you.

CREON. Now, now, Medea, no bartering, no blandishments!
Woman. (*Fumbling for his script.*) I have to banish you.
Here's where I say, 'Out of my city now! Go this instant!'

MEDEA. Dear gods above! And my children, too?

CREON. (*Abandoning his script and improvising.*)
Aye, take your brats with you. We want no bastards here.
Jason will father my own legitimate heir.
The noble Jason this morning wed my daughter.

NURSE. (*Sardonically.*) If we were lucky enough to be Greek
We would applaud your policy of ethnic cleansing.

CREON. And who deserves more fame in Greece than Jason?
Who steered the Argo through barbarian seas,
Laid siege to the hundred-headed dragon, drugged
Or slew it (I forget which) to retrieve the golden apples?

EURIPIDES. Fleece, Creon, *fleece*, not apples. Jason stole the Golden
Fleece.

CREON. (*Worked up in his role.*) Golden whatever.
I won't be side tracked by details. Who else but Jason,
Wrapped in a loincloth made of lion's skin,
Single-handedly strangled hellish Cerberus?

EURIPIDES. Not so! Hades' dog was choked by Herakles!

CREON. (In full spate.) Who threaded Daedalus's labyrinth
While fending off that sick witch, Ariadne?
Her he abandoned! (*To Medea.*) You were too strong for him.

(*Giggles from the cast and* CHORUS.)

EURIPIDES. Creon. You've simply got to learn your lines!

MEDEA. (*On her knees in operatic style.*)
Ah, Creon, I made strong magic once,
But I've forgotten my skills.
Weak, without means of defence,
I am abased, deserted. Every scalding hour
Seals my despair.
What will become of my little ones?
Who will give me shelter?
Divorcees are never welcome anywhere.
Oh yes, I'll go, I'll go without a murmur.
Where I have once been happy
I could never linger. I ask you only – one last kingly favour.
Give me a day, at least the remains of today,
To make my arrangements.
Creon, believe me, you have nothing to fear.
I can't just disappear!
O, find it in your heart to pity me, Creon!
Pity my children, and Jason's, dear to his heart.
Eight poor little working hours are all I want.

CREON. Medea, your words are honey, but your thoughts are gall.

MEDEA. So you don't trust me!

CREON. Not at all!

NURSE What harm could she do in half a day or less?

CREON. Once a murderess, always a murderess.
Will you go quietly or with soldiers at your side?

MEDEA. I beseech you! In the name of your daughter-bride!

CREON. Woman, you're wasting your breath and my time.

MEDEA. Why am I punished? Is love a crime?

CREON. Love? No. (*He laughs.*) It's because I love my family
*And* I love my country that I don't love you or yours.

MEDEA. Then there's no real love in your nature.
Love is the mother of pity.
If you were acquainted with love, you would grant my prayer.

CREON. Madam, no one has ever accused me of being unfair.
I want you out of Corinth, but I'm no tyrant.

If, as you say, you need time to pack and prepare,
I'll not prevaricate.
Look. The sun, by our shadows, stands just at noon.
If, when it appears so tomorrow, you're still here,
Abandon all hope for your life. It will be too late.

MEDEA *prostrates herself at* CREON's *feet as* CREON *gathers his robes around him muttering to himself as he departs.*

A mistake? A mistake. This may be a mistake.
I know I'm a sentimentalist, I can't help it.
Probably a mistake... (*Exit* CREON.)

MEDEA. (*Rising briskly.*) Well, that's that. Silly old dupe!
Do you think I'd have toadied to that idiot
If I hadn't needed time to set my trap?
Now, ladies, with twenty methods in my head,
Which shall I try first?

NURSE.                    The bridal bed.
Creep into the palace and set fire to it!

2ND CHORUS. No, too much smoke.
Consummate their marriage with your knife, instead!

MEDEA. I can't risk being seen at the palace.
If I were caught, I'd look ridiculous.
No, there's only one way. Poison.
Heavens, ladies, don't be squeamish. Come.
Gather round me. Remember who I am.
Medea! Nature's sorceress! Granddaughter of the Sun!
No more lamentations, no more tears!
My chronicle of vengeance has begun!

*Exit* MEDEA *and* CHORUS.


## SCENE II

*A garden could be suggested by a change of lighting. Enter* JASON, *stage left, as if playing ball with his sons, acting as if nothing had happened, to playful music.* EURIPIDES, *in the role of the boys' tutor, approaches* MEDEA *at stage right.*

EURIPIDES. Madam, your husband is with the children in the garden.

MEDEA. Jason? He dares to show his face?

EURIPIDES. He asks to see you, Madam.

61

MEDEA. And jeer at the spectacle of my disgrace?
Ah, there you are, slime-bag!
What do you want, you tube of intestinal gas?

JASON. Medea, please. I've come to offer you assistance.

MEDEA. Scum! What assistance can a nerd like you give me?

JASON. (*In jazz rhythm*.)
A man like me
Doesn't need a woman like you.
Why can't you see
These unladylike displays won't do?
You should, in propriety,
Accept what you're given with grace.
In civilised society
A woman has to know her place.
Although you won't believe me,
I'll always be your friend.
Be rational, dear lady,
And your imaginary grief will end.

MEDEA. Rational! I wonder the word
Doesn't blister your lying lips,
Incinerate your tongue
And singe the very air you breathe!
Worm! Limp as a worm! So you've come
To brave the she wolf in her den?
Ha, ha. Listen to him, ladies!
Jason, you know as well as I do
How I loved and saved you.
Who, when you failed to yoke my daddy's bulls,
Hexed them with her spells?
Who drugged, then knifed
The hundred-headed beast
That coiled with lidless eyes around the fleece?
And all because I was mad, mad, mad for you!
You, who promised we would make our bed on it –
As we did, remember,
Night after night under the stars. (*She sobs*.)

JASON. You forget that when we met, Madam,
You were a goat-skin princess
Sleeping on a hard, clay floor.
Savage as a beast, you were,

Hardly fit to be called human.
A painted whore, a witchy girl
No Greek gentleman would look at twice.
Of course, you were of use to me
In that awkward business of the Golden Fleece.
I watched you, and I washed you,
Knowing I'd have to play the price.

MEDEA. Are you suggesting that you never loved me?

JASON. No. Just that your fingernails weren't nice.

MEDEA. Gods! Do you hear him and let him live?

JASON. I've always found your energy attractive.
I let you cling. Let you do anything.
Stood by you when you chopped your brother
Into butcher's meat to gain a day...

MEDEA.                                    Never!

JASON. Against my principles, that sort of thing.
But thanks to you, the Argo got away.

MEDEA. And what about your wicked uncle, Jason?
Who persuaded me to cancel him?
Oh, Jason, all my killings were for you!
And all you've done for me you now undo.

JASON. (*Changing tack.*) Medea, I don't deny it! You've been useful
to me.
A clever girl. A good mother, too.
Together, here in Corinth, we've not done badly.
I don't regret our marriage, not at all.
But now I can't afford to act selfishly.
I have to consider my children.

MEDEA. YOUR children!

JASON. Our children. Think what this royal marriage can do for
them.
With princes for siblings, consider their options for success.

MEDEA. Success? When they're stuck with me in exile?

JASON. All might have been otherwise, my dear,
Had you behaved sensibly.
This house, its luxuries, its servants,
All could have been yours.

But no, you reverted to curses,
Terrifying Creon, alienating my bride,
But hurting – listen to me! – mainly yourself!

MEDEA. Heaven preserve me!

CHORUS. She doesn't want your property!
She won't accept your presents!
She doesn't need your friends!

MEDEA. By all the gods, Jason,
I curse you. I curse you. I'll never forgive you.
Believe me, I'll have my revenge.

JASON. That's just what I'm afraid of, Medea, my dear.
That's why you will pack up NOW and be gone.

MEDEA. Shoo! Shoo! Be gone yourself.
Your beautiful bride awaits you!
A feast is spread in your bridal bed!
Wowee! You disgust me!
A woman like me
Doesn't need a man like you.
Just wait and see
What a woman like me can do!

JASON. Pig-ignorant, bone-headed, self-destructive bitch!
(*To the Chorus.*) Time's running out on her. What can she do?

*Exit* JASON.


## SCENE III

EURIPIDES, *script in hand, leads* MEDEA *and the* CHORUS *on stage,
placing them for his version of the play.* MEDEA *reluctantly follows*
EURIPIDES' *instructions.*

EURIPIDES. (*Lecturing.*) Trust the script. Trust the immortal script.
This is the classical scene that made my name.
Play it my way, and it will make yours, too.

MEDEA. (*Furiously.*) I know, I know, I know what I shall do!

1ST CHORUS. Careful Medea. Strong feelings like yours
Never do any good.

2ND CHORUS. A tempered passion, like a gentle voice,
Brings its own reward.

NURSE. To satisfy your violent love for Jason
You sacrificed your father and your home.
Don't let your violent hatred now
Antagonise the friends who might protect you.

MEDEA. (*To* EURIPIDES.) Why all this tedious moralising?

EURIPIDES. The Greeks liked it.
Besides, 'protect you' is King Aegeus's cue.

CREON, *doubling as the disguised* KING AEGEUS *of Athens, pulls off his beard and diadem, drapes himself in a travelling cloak from the costume box and looks around for his staff.*

CREON/AEGEUS. Coming, coming. I seem to have lost my stick!

MEDEA. I don't think we're going to need you, Aegeus.
Would you mind if we cut this scene?

CREON/AEGEUS. Cut my scene? Why yes, I would mind.
I'm being paid, you know, to play both kings.
Apart from that, I'm crucial to the plot.
On my way back from the oracle at Delphi
I meet you, weeping on the road from Corinth.
You tell me Jason's deserted you.
I tell you I am old, without an heir.
You put it to me that if I give you a home,
You'll see to it that I have a son.
The arrangement suits us both.

MEDEA. Yes, But nothing like that happened.
I never went to Athens.
I never was Aegeus' whore.
(*To* EURIPIDES.)
You're not the only bard who spread that rumour!

2ND CHORUS. You mean the classics tell lies?

EURIPIDES. Well, a poet is most himself when he invents.
What's any story without... ornaments?

MEDEA. Of course, I don't object to creativity. But no one
Has damaged my reputation so much
As you, Euripides, who made me murder my sons!

JASON. Glauke and Creon? Did you murder them?

MEDEA. Possibly. (*Glaring at* EURIPIDES.)
But not the way he says I did!

JASON. Tell us, Medea. In your own words confess:
Did you or did you not send my bride a poisoned dress.

MEDEA. This much is true. I was jealous of Glauke.
I wanted her dead.
I wanted to poison her and Jason in their bed.
With no way to slip into the palace,
I remembered my wedding dress –
A gift from my grandfather, the Sun.

(*From the costume box she tenderly lifts out a golden robe.*)

Now, for a woman of my race and colour,
A gown like this is a guarantee of power.
Look how it gilds and glorifies my skin!
For a pale, pathetic little runt like Glauke
It was certain death. Not from poison!
She wouldn't have died that night or the next day.
Had all gone as planned, I'd have been far away
By the time that subatomic radiation
Worked its way into her bloodstream.
She would have sickened slowly. And when she died,
No one in the world would have known why.

JASON. You are a devil, Medea.
You deserve damnation!

MEDEA. But my dress never killed her.
It didn't kill Creon.
They died because I cried for the sun.
Down he came in his fiery chariot and bore me away!
Euripides, let's continue with the play.

*The* CHORUS *and cast assemble again, centre stage.*

1ST CHORUS. Oh Zeus, master of the life-giving sun,
Strike down this demon-driven woman
Before she wields her knife against her children.

2ND CHORUS. Stay her, stop her, divine God of Light!
Rid this house of a creature possessed,
Helpless in the power of her revenge.

*As the* CHORUS *moves, singing and dancing,* MEDEA *retreats into the
house. There are cries from within.*

1ST CHORUS. Vain is the labour you have spent on your children.

66

In vain you gave birth to healthy sons.
Unhappy woman, I fear all the Furies possess you!

2ND CHORUS. Cries! Listen! Piteous shrieks for help!
What can we do to check the slaughter?
Shall I force the door and enter?

*Enter* JASON, *sword in hand, eager to avenge the deaths of* GLAUKE
*and* CREON.

JASON. Women and all who weep by this accursèd house,
Know that Medea has murdered your king and my bride.
Is the murderess here? Is she hiding inside?
Vengeance is in the air. I fear for my children.

NURSE. Oh Jason, unhappy man,
More and worse sorrows pursue you.
Your children are dead. Dead by their mother's hand!

JASON. Dead? My boys? Dead, you say. Both gone?
Unmerciful gods! How? Where? Can she have killed them?

NURSE. Open the door and you will see.

JASON *forces open the door but no bodies are revealed. Instead,* MEDEA
*steps boldly out on the balcony with her two sons. (These could be dolls.)*

MEDEA. Lies, Euripides, lies. It's, you, you who are the murderer.
You, with your tricks of rhetoric, have killed my sons!

EURIPIDES. Shut up, Medea! What are you?
A figment of my imagination, no more!
A fiction of my genius for poetry!

MEDEA. Oh Mother Nature, Creator of earth and sky,
Receive and defend me!
Father Helios, Great Emperor of Heaven,
Descend and preserve me!

*As* MEDEA *raises her arms in prayer, the light increases on the stage to
an almost unbearable intensity. A wind storm rises and sweeps through
the scenery, toppling the canvas city – a tornado, an earthquake. The
devastation brought about by this natural disaster has to be suggested
by wild music.*

CHORUS & CAST. (*Wailing, trying to escape.*) Ai! Ai! Ai!

MEDEA. My sons! My sons! Euripides, save my sons!

## SCENE IV

*The Underworld. Blackout. A curtain falls to hide the wrecked set. After some minutes of total silence, the lights slowly brighten to suggest the perpetual twilight of Hades. On a bare stage, a spotlight reveals* MEDEA, *prostrate at stage right. Slowly she lifts her head and comes to life as the music of her first aria revives her.*

MEDEA. The pain, the pain, I cannot bear the pain.
    What wife, deserted and betrayed, could bear such pain…
        (*She breaks off and look around at the empty set.*)
    How? Where? What's happened? Jason!
    (*Terrified.*) Jason! J-a-s-o-n!

*A second spotlight finds* JASON *prostrate, stage left. As* MEDEA *calls him he wakes and sleepily consults his wristwatch. He shakes it. It seems not to be working. He shakes it again, taps it, brings it to his ear, then impatiently rips it from his wrist and tosses it away. Rising, he rubs his chin and looks around for shaving things.* MEDEA *runs to him and throws herself in his arms.*

MEDEA. Jason, Jason, what's happened? Where are we?
    Where are the children? What have I done?

JASON. (*Disengaging himself.*) What have you done?
    Landed us in Hades, that's what you've done!

MEDEA. Hades?

JASON. Don't be coy, Medea. Don't play the innocent.
    Your crimes echo through history.
    You've killed us all: Creon, Glauke, me, the children.
    Along with yourself.

MEDEA. I? Killed us?

JASON. You. Who else could summon the sun
    To incinerate a city?

MEDEA. So that's what it was. I was too powerful.
    Death was my punishment.
    Jason, forgive me.
    We are dead, and our children are dead.
    And this Nothing, this sunless Nowhere, is Hades!

MEDEA *sinks down, weeping. Delighted by this sign of weakness,* JASON *lays a hand on her shoulder.*

JASON. Never mind, Medea, we'll pull through this somehow.
By Hades, I could do with some coffee and a shower.

*Enter* EURIPIDES, *dressed as a modern director, with two polystyrene cups of steaming coffee.* JASON *and* MEDEA *seize them eagerly as* EURIPIDES *settles himself in a director's chair set up for him, mid stage.*

EURIPIDES. Milk? Sugar? And immortality, too?

JASON. Immortality? In this ghastly hole?

EURIPIDES. Why yes. Only the dead are immortal.
Don't fret yourselves about your children.
They'll always be part of the show.
The afterlife is not a place, it's a performance,
Created, ahem, by celebrated poets like me.

MEDEA. There you go, Euripides, grabbing the credit!
But it was for me that the sun descended!

EURIPIDES. Nonsense. No one can hitch a ride with the sun.

JASON. Well, then, tell us what happened, Euripides.

MEDEA. Yes, you tell us Euripides.
Why did the city perish? Go on, you tell us!

(*As* EURIPIDES *begins to explain,* CREON, *the* NURSE *and rest of the cast slips onto the stage. Gradually the lights grow brighter.*)

EURIPIDES. (*Shrugging.*) It could have been an earthquake.

JASON.         An earthquake!

EURIPIDES.         Or a hurricane;
Something to do with the weather, anyway.
Nothing to do with you, I'm glad to say.
The music of time doesn't play for the dance of humanity.

MEDEA. Cock and bull! It's your own play, Euripides.
The sun comes down to rescue me in your own play!

(*Inarticulate with fury,* MEDEA *hurls her coffee at* EURIPIDES.)

EURIPIDES. (*Brushing his trousers.*) Mythical coffee, my dear,
It doesn't stain.

JASON. (*Excited, interrupting.*) Listen, Medea,
If everyone in Corinth perished naturally,
Then you didn't kill your children!

69

An earthquake lets you off the hook completely!
You're exonerated. Clean as a Christian. Guilt free!

MEDEA. Hear that, Euripides? Guilt free!

CHORUS. Guilt free! Guilt free! Guilt free!

EURIPIDES. Not so fast, not so fast!
Without your guilt, my dear,
You wouldn't be worth mythologising.

CREON. Besides, you have to answer for a crime
More serious than murder: Hubris –
Pride of mind, disrespect for the sublime.

MEDEA. Pride of mind? Disrespect for the sublime?
Who's disrespectful of heaven if not Euripides?
He thinks the gods are figments of his mind.

CHORUS. (*With* MEDEA, *mocking* EURIPIDES.)
He doesn't believe in the gods.
He doesn't believe in me!
He thinks we're made of words!
He thinks the world is made of words!

EURIPIDES. Never! If words were gods,
I'd keep all heaven and earth in fun and games.

(*Silence, as* EURIPIDES *continues a little cynically.*)

I'm only a sort of manufacturer, you know.
I never claimed to own the factory.
I never claimed that what I wrote was true.
No, friends, I was hired to entertain.
If you don't approve my fancies, let them go!

MEDEA. Oh, let's get this show on the road, for heaven's sake.
Ye gods, wherever you are, whoever you are,
Deliver us from Hades!
OK. I'll make a deal with you, Euripides!
I'll give up my sun-daddy for your earthquake,
If you'll let me off murdering my boys!

(EURIPIDES *and* MEDEA, *suspicious still, shake hands.*)

JASON. Wait a minute, wait a minute.
I'm not sure I like this.
If you've been making up stories –
Either one of you – I sure do resent it!

If Nature destroyed Corinth, where were the gods?
Sir, I sincerely believe in my religion.
I was a believer all my life. I was a hero.
I have to know my gods were great and true.

EURIPIDES. Well, if that's what you need to know, the only way
Is to start again at the beginning of the play.
Everybody here? Medea, Jason, Nurse, Chorus,
Take your places please.

*The back curtain rises revealing a film of a modern city with glass sky-*
*scrapers, dazzling lights, busy throughways, pylons, cranes, etc.* JASON,
MEDEA, EURIPIDES *and the rest assemble, rummaging for costumes in*
*the costume box as before.* EURIPIDES *relocates his scripts and passes*
*them around. The* NURSE *reopens the play:*

NURSE. Oh that the Argo had never slipped through the Clashing
        Rocks
To beach at Colchis, that Pelion's virgin pines
Had never been hacked down for oars!
Then would Medea be a mighty queen in Colchis,
Not powerless in Corinth, weakened by marriage to Jason...

*The* NURSE*'s recitation fades as* EURIPIDES *and* MEDEA *advance to*
*the footlights together. Music continues as they divide the last speech in*
*Euripides' original tragedy.*

EURIPIDES. Many things do the gods accomplish unexpectedly.

MEDEA. Often that which was hoped for does not occur.

EURIPIDES. Yet the powers that control the planet find a way
Of bringing the unforeseen to pass.

MEDEA. And so it happened here.

*A slow drum beat (or other appropriate music) ends the play.*

Anne Stevenson was born in Cambridge, England, in 1933, of American parents, and grew up in New England and Michigan. She studied music, European literature and history at the University of Michigan, returning later to read English and write the first critical study of Elizabeth Bishop. After several transatlantic switches, she settled in Britain in 1964, and has since lived in Cambridge, Scotland, Oxford, the Welsh Borders and latterly in North Wales and Durham. She has held many literary fellowships, and was the inaugural winner of Britain's biggest literary prize, the Northern Rock Foundation Writer's Award, in 2002.

As well as her numerous collections of poetry, Anne Stevenson has published a biography of Sylvia Plath (1989), a book of essays, *Between the Iceberg and the Ship* (1998), and two critical studies of Elizabeth Bishop's work, most recently *Five Looks at Elizabeth Bishop* (Bloodaxe Books, 2006). Her latest poetry books are *Poems 1955-2005* (2005) and *Stone Milk* (2007), both from Bloodaxe.